Closet Haikus

A Letter from The Author

About three years ago, I began writing about my own experience "coming out of the closet." I sought to do so in a way that created community and started conversations.

Naturally, playing with form became a priority, and I begin exploring moments of my coming out process through haikus. It's an approachable form and is suitable for both the serious and hilarious parts of coming out.

After about thirty haikus had been written, I found myself doubting the project.

Who was I to tell this story?

Using the powers of the internet and the LGBTQ+ community and its allies, I sought to collect coming out stories, which I could turn into haikus and publish in a collaborative poetry collection.

The Closet Haikus Kickstarter campaign was launched on April 15, 2019. With the support of 57 backers, Closet Haikus was fully funded just five short weeks later.

Now, Closet Haikus is out in the world.

Thank you to the following backers for supporting and believing in this project:

Rosalie C., Annabel G., Katie S., Victoria B., Lizelle van Vuuren, Alyssa San Diego., Emily S., Weston N., Beth B., Haley, Ellen Grace, Sara & Sam H., Ash S., Lissette C., H.J., Robyn D., Melissa H., Dyke Haiku, Cait, Scott

T., Christina & Taren Stanton, Adrienne H., Anonymous, David R., James P., Edie A., Alison B., Sarah S., Em, Laura B., Ellie J., Sierra G., Abby & Andrea, Arella, Doug M., Megan L., Tyler N., Stephanie W., Molly, Tessa L., Rand F., Bly, Rachel G., Karley, DjiEm, Cynthia, Joe B., Laurie D., Francesca K., William R., Zyla, Lindsay M., Scott B.

I hope that this project turns into even more. That this collection of pieces nudges others to share their stories, and that many editions of this project will follow.

For now, I hope you enjoy this collaborative coming out poetry collection – the first of its kind.

For anyone who would like to participate in the future, please email me at ClosetHaikus@gmail.com.

Thank you all!

Rachel. R. Noall

Closet Haikus

I baked my message.
Airy and decorated.
We smiled and ate.

- For Ellie J.

Can girls have short hair?
Yes. Short like my patience when
People assume things.

- For Laura B.

On graduation
I proudly wore a dress.
I was supported.

- For Anonymous

Steadfast in knowing
Fluidity is freeing
Like your open arms.

-For Em

We make choices to
Learn so we can be better.
Live in the present.

-For Alison B.

Outed by a text,
I became a warrior
And conquered the beast.

- For Edie A.

It comes out in waves
Like the rhythm of our vows
To Niagara's rush.

- For James P.

Life at work concealed
I share my they/them pronouns
They thanked me – progress.

- For Cait

An Easter egg hunt
For me, the missing daughter.
Coming out was hard.

- For Dyke Haiku

A lonely quiet
In our home after the news
I've had crushes.

- For H.J.

A midnight story
After dropping years of hints
20 and ready.

- For Ellen Grace

"What will my friends think?"
A weight lifted alone but
It made me strong.

- For Haley

A locker room dream.
She and I standing, kissing.
I woke up happy.

- For Emily S.

True love from the start
We lived and grew together.
I am so lucky.

- For Sara and Sam H.

Happy to be me.
Crying scared at the same time.
Surprise, I am bi.

- For Anonymous

I cried hard that night
Fearing a loss of family.
A bond unbroken.

- For Ash S.

The guru had "it"
Not just makeup moved me.
Renewed and whole.

- For Melissa H.

Written out or known
Love is affirmed unspoken.
A balance that works.

- For Christina and Taren

With a drink in hand
I stand before a large crowd
And yell it loudly.

- For Anonymous

Questions to answer
A night out, a secret wish.
Always on my mind.

- For David R.

I dropped the news
On a soothing road trip home.
Emma Watson crush.

- For Alyssa San Diego

We found common ground
In fun Black & Mild tears.
Friendship at its best.

- For Weston N.

Just started T Shots.
I knew HR could help me.
It made me feel safe.

-For Anonymous

A small town, afraid.
Everything could change.
It went really well.

- For Adrienne H.

I took down some walls
And came out to me − courage.
A tattoo helped.

- For Sarah S.

I see the caution.
An ally undercover,
For those needing it.

- For Scott T.

A Catholic campus.
I spoke my truth to many,
I helped them feel safe.

- For Annabel Gong

"I like dogs not cats."
The culture of coming out.
Why must we explain?

- For Beth Birchfield

To confide and thrive.
Tears between laughter.
Don't sacrifice yourself.

- For Rosalie Candau

So many questions.
My finger on the button.
Looking for women.

- For Katie Silasiri

A high school love.
A stepping stone towards truth.
Maybe I helped her.

- For Victoria Barrios

Speaking champagne truths
A weight was lifted off.
Everlasting love.

- For Lizelle van Vuuren

Can we dance all night?
A prom I wouldn't forget.
I told my parents.

-For Anonymous

The End

Made in the USA
Columbia, SC
02 January 2024

29726455R00024